PINK NOISE

KEVIN
HOLDEN

PINK
NOISE

NIGHTBOAT
BOOKS

NEW YORK

COPYRIGHT © 2023 BY KEVIN HOLDEN

ALL RIGHTS RESERVED
PRINTED IN THE UNITED STATES

ISBN: 978-1-643-62177-7

DESIGN AND TYPESETTING BY KIT SCHLUTER
TYPESET IN PERPETUA

CATALOGING-IN-PUBLICATION DATA IS AVAILABLE FROM
THE LIBRARY OF CONGRESS

NIGHTBOAT BOOKS
NEW YORK
WWW.NIGHTBOAT.ORG

Contents

For Michael

mica

that would a
creek drank
or certainty through
& objects contracting
vertices of xs
a hardwood to shower
his
rippling
& tender that would be
& go up the cliff
lone pine atop it
that would be a lilac bush
him running past you
turning into lilacs

riot

the streets at night

& is a circle or queer sapphire ringing plastic
o young man fabulous muscles star & it
is a dark shadow flowing over pines
a store nearby showering grey sparks
I found you in a club circling in air
it was, they say, your mind or
down the walls really leading
a corner laughing or nebulous darling
cumulus rocking stones over broken statue
a dirt pond mouthing in golden archangel
the norm cannot compete with that color

When I was younger I wore only one color. My boyfriend liked
to fuck in parking lots. We used to go to these reeds by a lake.
He was kind of punk but had the most beautiful sweaters.

After the protests the police held us for a very long time. He
was avoiding their questions but looking very directly into their
eyes. This bothered them & so they hit him.

red
gold
radii

so we left the green
housing project
to go to
the sea

glass, heaping, hyaline waves

so cold today

then at night a piece of meat booking it, ashen heaps
'werqit in da cold' she says
over those scraps, hot boys hustling in the snow

inverted triangles, angelic swarms, bread

we are dancing to 'goodbye horses' in the dark
outside there is so much snow in the darkness
we burn a cardboard box in the middle of the wooden floor
we dance and drink and kiss and jump
seraphs in white leather jackets
'goodbye horses, I'm dying over you'

when we left we were harassed, someone threw a rock

all motion and no motion
freedom and sex are seeds
arching becoming chariots

so cold today

we are writing this down because they are acts & to grip something of the world

5^2 / a sunflower

this is Time Square
42nd st

ribboning out numerically wandering happily tie down to the bed tied up to a railroad tie splintered the heavier flowers

went all the way wanted to see was the tall buildings today is blue if right gay is still young suicide & black shirt pink flag palindrome they say walk fag into the tub it is there for you

      boy top blond sun hard
      green shame at garden edge wall
      end on within self itself
      hard white sheer body boundary
      sub boy meth blows lab

We were wandering. We were arguing. This was a group of concerned citizens. This was a group that thought it needed protection & change & light & a window I thought we needed a window if we say something different then good every flower would overflow a grammar our union wanted to say something about assemblages there is this whole set of losses chalking salting gathering weight bits of broken salt metal anyway exactly you understand.

his tastes like a tree
or it tastes of moss and wet bark
or metal and lichen
his body this vegetal mineral thing

you there you had breathed in coal dust & that is something,
we are seeing there is a solidity of the group itself this cluster
of agents of windows and trash-scapes the function the things
that are silenced & this a position for the speaking it out

twelvetone to him his sugared root
as rock or quartz or smoke hung with
branches, golddust rung with sunshafts

and we walk back together through the leaf strewn streets
in our shades of flannel
and are beat
up for
holding hands

that then caused queer flowering in pink
lattices shouldering up a bunch of them fighting in the street holding
an intersection
tear gas cascading in rainbows across their bleary eyes

you want to fight a city
zigzagging heap lightyear in a dark function and any kind of rhythm,
damn you, we wanted to bust them open talking about money and they
clear cut the whole thing

and streams flow
wild song standing therefore
listen voices silver leaves
monarch, broken root, crushed can
money rustles in the throats of the wealthy
in autumn the insect
always shores up against so
allium grit make him hard
to bend to have to skin

or my friend, a great poet, who said for a long time she had trouble
with activism against the police, because they are also workers, also
trapped within a system that is capitalism or class or militarized
government, and then she wrote a poem that said ——

because you get to make a choice

under him bullets backyard quiver
cup held for loose change
painted sugar along street atoms
hose crowd cop street spray

soup from an ashtray
I mean, shred
you the beautiful
barn or fragrant
rhinestones / eyelashes
we to say, by the project
asphodel under there, you couldn't stay there
or running prisons privately
against the vile megaphone flame
this
trace
shimmer on a rooftop quaking
those men, eat glass

and so his death was not so the others could appreciate their own lives

not so that they could come to a meaning & place

this is not a film

you can't see
yourself

or fall in line

now it might be happening through the populace

reels of action projected through the trees
aspen genus, people moving

one might say,
an array of
pink triangles

if something appears
fierce queen on a blank stage

a slab of quartz in the snow
a sort of directed rage

crown yellow winter older gear
cop hit lie mother yelling
kid lot dirt rock kick
happy striped blue tent breaking
circle tetris genius flower chrome

yellow bandages in a bunch for a mesh inside
the diamonds crushed, in your lover's heart, bashed up and hungry
then into any backlit room or flopped diadem a bunch of homos sleeping

so you would say unfolding any dark dream she had under the back
porch take a walk on the wild lady came to play flowing dries into
hidden spaces two songs running over one another penetrating in
perfect bright striations

to act up to act up

and the heaping up of acts you walk through accumulating
distances or thought of blush infinities
the groundwork strewn with work and choice

so shattered into stilettoed loop of angelic armies
to spread their lovers' ashes on the White House lawn

remember a lover smoking on a rooftop
across a rooftop shadowing the anarchists
astral carpets blurring in the smoke

the gauge is high
we might climb up

and over endless mesh and identities
strung in deep sound or hope
and/or
long talk at empire's close

flung free under all the snow
to widen endlessly in padded violently
he breaks out to say, come outside

so if we move up
& people in the street this could be
this as a burning floe
at the end of a curve
roll out in a bright dress naked at the door

grit

•

other stuff about cities
pinecone, snow studies

ovum, foam
dactyl, fractal, spar

and chasing ice

ice town, ghost town

one plus one equals
one

sick ward, cots, lead
in white plaster
and string, the white paint

all the dead names in grey combinatoric
the unborn
filled with water

dandelion mixen seeded

snow studies queer topological manifold
cold black cellophane cicada caryatid in the diamond mine
or grasshopper green strip mall

city / sidewalk
suburb / lawns
dumpster under bridge / puffy coats
other stuff about cities
subways / glass buildings / fountains / the poor / guns
and border Nuuk & Alert etc.

goodly mica

to do that sex work
glass pane shards planes
in a cloth book

•

that so all the colors in the ice feather
to think about the natural world
not the polis, the poles not the polis
and there is a reason for that

color hearing your thought fixed in a vice
in the sound hold so foursquare in the
filaments bent make a sound hole
light swimming upward through the swimming
hole the prisms and iridescent darknesses beyond
showering and falling down the sinkhole
four rivers and glasses and birds

that to say or ask which side of the mirror
are you on, so the logic flows backward

multiple suns, that would be

that is, unconceal heaven

land in sidereal starfield turn left
unattended to hear music too loud to hear
dilating and contracting, the sound sea
pale white light captured on the side of the square
fading but brightening

•

to say or remember the mine or sounding
the depth of the mineshaft the shadows
that we forget (in order) to move from one
word to the next — that we must forget in order
to do so — so we would be all
presence — that would be — and all that
word — never moving — plus the other —
meaning, if we didn't — that is — all the words
would stack up, would accumulate, would
pile up in an endless heap to trail along forever
unrevolving — to static — or,
that we must forget
to do so — that is — to remember
not to move — or deeper — to forget about
moving — strip oneself, more, fall
away — forget even
forgetting — so we stay in the one
presencing to grow —
or snow snow snow

tunnel

I

Events,
that were not real,
were collecting
in the streams
of my and others'
day. As though
the hollowness
had never been
under us. And
the landscape
had always been
like this. And green.
I, likewise.
Propagated
and green, the moths
pressed against
the panes, maybe
in the hope
that they would
get into our system.
Water was dripping
from our schematics.
Pooling in blue
just like our day.
A system was to be
found in this

they insisted.
As though
they were aware
of my privates.
My smock
and my workbench
and my ruler.
I'm not sure
what to think
anymore I said
to my distribution
supervisor
in the barn
under the
fluorescents.
He just
looked at me
faceless
like always,
like a piece
of tungsten.
I sighed and
continued
my work on the rain.

II

Later,
the workers
in the dim blue
light of the barn
felt a collective
shudder as if

as they say
someone walked over
your grave.
The light
was lowered.
On an angle,
if it was possible,
the condensation
of dreams
transpired in the
tensile,
rudimentary light
of the orb.
War-ships
were there
and the workers
cleaned the grit
from the stream.
They must
have been aware of
my thought pattern
in the lab
for the perfection
of the weather,
the rain.

III

The barn
has cedar shingles
and some horsehair.
Its porch chairs
have holes

in their seats.
Math and moths
collecting
at the exits,
near the on-ramp.
We were all uncertain
about the water,
a shift
that was visible
in the reality
of our tactile
& radial grid.
The winds and
false trees.
My supervisor,
though he
has no face,
looks distrustful
and powerful
over his clipboard,
like an idiot,
like someone
who is going
to destroy me.
The rain has
been dripping
for days,
and we can't
stop it
though we
lift our hands daily
to our rainy collars
and eyes.

IV

Our barn
is full of moths
beating against
the dust-caked
bulbs. Dirt
is also caked
on the screen-door
and it smells
like dirt on a screen.
I feel around
when the light is off
looking for a mouth
or the rain button
which I am
supposed to push
even in the dark
which is both
the war and reality
of our clear
civilization.
And the moths
agree with their
arcs, the cedar
glinting
in rubber/tidal
arrows, and plastic,
dirt-water rim
pulling on my privates.
The barn
stands glowing
and clear in the night
like so much

circuitry.
It is glowing
like winter.
Like ghosts.
Later,
the other workers
remove my smock
and fuck me at night,
but so gently.
Then
I am pure
algorithm.
Once
one of them
while inside me
and arcing
whispered,
like a cave of winds,
Ezekiel,
you feel
like a cave
of warm glass.
Thank you,
I said, watching
the rain.

polytopes

Moreover, I turned then to examine the nature of the mind, but the false opinion which I held about spiritual entities did not allow me to perceive the truth. The truth with great force leapt to my eyes, but I used to turn away my agitated mind from incorporeal reality to lines and colors and physical magnitudes of vast size. Because I could not see any such thing in the mind, I thought I could not see my mind.

—AUGUSTINE

Compare the phenomenon of thinking with the phenomenon of burning.

—WITTGENSTEIN

nephilim

antiphonal twelve
tone as if there
could be such a thing
anticomb the pollen
a yellow shivering
to take your
seraphim & synapses
the spaces between oh
a raven a crow an owl
show me the backside
of the databarn
1 Yottabyte of brain
oh come on now
you would say super
computer cum on my face

boolean

endless hours opening
a field flung in dark roses
slowing it is not a
hinge flowing
snowing
the snow, upon snow
branches infinitely in bark

it could be boolean
those 361 versions of change
your mascara clacking down the gearshaft
do you remember the busdriver all in numbers
these red tables for blue picnics
or, see the world
1,000 things all aglow or sparking feldspar
aleuromancer in finite powders bluster
love us all a polychoron in there

chrysoprase

rhombicubicosachoron the antipodal
variation for Vyvyan &
wheels within wheels take him
from behind thrusting in infinite
variation the god splits in two
& is in front & is behind, this
perfect green man, cut out of
wood, anyway ophanim, the
darker substrate a Subway
McDonald's a Wendy's at 3 AM
in the wastes of the city
come out of the club
enter the electric grid
ECT shivering up through her spine
& digitizing thunder
& traffic noises
say again rainbow rainbow
all the music
is a rainbow

hyaline plains

that would any
I heap in glassy mathematics
shiver into a corner
black and white go, strung over grid
little bowls
you to show any stellation in here

please be my
blue redux for aqueduct labeling
you shout dark nibelung
I'd say
happy opaque quartz a shouting

all those plains
ever darkling in it
blacken your ore into transfinite huge glyph
white aleph burning into you
taste that salt
at the starry edge now

we weep into happy cubes
feet untethered but aimless, vectoralist
you shower in rosy shadows
poetry is the negative
space of being

in it all folded ligaments shower
vortex for the fistful flowers

back in it for you j curve
we are here
saddened in those multiformdances
flow out
in a dress of graphemes open at the door

megaspace

that would say onyx rigel system comb
unanswered paper cranes following a chord
mocked child sitting at the counter
or a purpleshadow tricycle found at the corner
enough of that the old lady says
either a dandelion or lionphlox
it goes in endless grains a terrace in the project
above the rafters loan in an interest a dark interest
stab the bully up under the porch
mint yellow sissy blow through the edging poppies
bright green syrup chrysoprase in a strong cylinder
it would mean
to be outside
to be the strongest & crush it
to summon ghosts
o that, a chip on your shoulder
fly out above the dissonant chimetune
little whining phone
the blue chip radiating braided auras
o a rounder cube . . . hustling in the snow
a piece of meat booking it, potato heaps
over those scraps hot boys hustling in the snow

peridot

awaken each moment in an emerald cube
and see that scene of transmutation that
metamorphosis or phosphorescent blur
point being be inside the point of light
lit a rhizome to be it then
greener algorithm in his mind
bones in his white sheen
bulge in his white jeans
veins in his big arms
regardless Hegel saw the pyramids as vast prisms of death
regardless Vishnu reclines on a sea of milk
"the sky milk-blue and astringent" he says
"the snow is a different color out here; blue; like skim milk" he says
why we recline on this day as opposed to others
the world is all that / we must pass over in silence
antichoron flame up in his mind
this Styx and null set
recombine to a vision of your life behind bars
an ever darkening infinity
so you break it apart
with your bare bloody hands
and thank your mother for your name

cyanide foam

ander rock salt cliff fiscality
those dark fish would quiver
lift off you say counting ever downward redshifting
labellunglief should follow suit
hexagram in an ace of spades gaining size

shadow trains lightning box would shower or spark
in cages or urethane
mind a bear trap haha
being blackblue carrot emperor
see that cascade of empty rhythms
lang outside music
la la any force through your brainvector la

keep dancing feel a felled tree
those heavy trunks

we had dreams of our old school
that old skill
kill the fish heavy homo
fall in line
scattered in pink gut

llll would show that screen
anemic glass plate
shoved up there

nanospace

la jar regional arcturus laughing lit up
that a ton or blue dancer in under
following under to stay there & learn cavernous
a pear blowing furious in street cavernous
that would darling education her to say
not a hungry proposal authority to the other
it is true to wait an endless march in greyer circles
flow a following baptized Japanese flower
the book flows not a space in this country lemonclouded
an apple tree if you like, a following over coffee a church exactly e
a hungry after x-ward
pink delirium under darker quadrature
flee a following
dandelion storm
you to say leaderboard, motherboard
eeny meeny miny mo deep square la
wet coffee for you at sunrise w/ hematite
sing a lovely tune Catherine & the mountains
or a shadow puppy rolling in woods
sooo late a kid stumbles home
'werqit in da cold' says V
in the oak milk
the grain in wood seeking granular
through sugarmesh or, he came a dark storm

azeotrope

howling clarity
or akashic field
rose tone row you say or sorry
I mizz you so showering cedar
& dusk has 8oo eyes to rainbow matrices link us
happy lattice theory
~~or scotch tape keeping in~~
being flow up in lilac bruise
squeak cluster drop
a drink to make sleep tiny
or mouse across the foot all around a blooming
heather field shower your cyber voiced plane
sad sad, go go

aves

transform that space
well, you're okay how
much money did
you get purple sage
field he'd say it
was real well I
don't remember that fold
a flock of geese in
triangles I'll give you
20 that would be
what the birds start with

lyotropic series

a violet moving in breezes
recombinant blue β cardinal oxidase
calcium or to say indigo rubixcube dream
a flowing toward dark infinity
human comedy flowing blackly
you to say, an index
~~charting dandelion phlox~~
twisted gay a deeper sex
or say, aleatoric television
wander derivatively Kant infinite regress
showing, clue cube cough cough
oxalis & slow
asterism overfoldingtriangle we eat ever
one would hope, a world x'd
nothing left in a sad country
sad or mad queers making noise
him one say lattice fugue
head or heart & we walk over
those fields & search ever for
a window frame for the world and
something tracing a ladder something something
and you say
leave that there for quartet for the
end of time, a polyhedron reading the accounts
voice shrill in endless crescendo
building in language games or

heaps of shells
& a burial mound
tumbling outward toward the sea
speaks the number in grey glass
speaks the number in white glass

pond tithe

repeat would rise deer summit
aleator tower yellow on an island
for lines staircase low in crystal
open shoulder for a patchwork
black asphodel you would, or among
redux the bounty & a homeless can on fire
flung . . . faggot under all the snow
to whiten endlessly in padded violently
break free you say antiphonal aleuro
he to say cum in flour
or, I love you
any math shower for a long time
people in the street this could be
this as
an island floe
you seering blue / shifting deer tarry
to see in endless
cut a cube hole through snow and
footthicklakeice a window
the waveless still or, quiet parlor
same sand as ever, those white grains
us or into something in graphite oblong stair
or, way

halcyon

you'd say a long time & the motion perpetual
parahelix for a day break a
rebus a rhombus a tisket a tasket
head of Orpheus in a wicker basket

cornflower

return that crisper grey square
in an emerald light
or lightning bug
in allotropic variety
for a queen & a castle
8 x 8 & a series of planned permutations
set from the start & a winter flower
five points of the folded star
mustardseed, goldenyield
hand hurting in another mind
your limits of being
pulled over onto the other sphere
lichen, birch a phenomenal ray
that nonspace by the board
his hands
or the lilac bush
that's what happened to me

dihedral prime

softer preposition in a backward loop
for Christian or Dorian or Lucifer
wingèd on the wind a beautiful boy
blond locks sing out over the river square
sit this one out the admiral may whisper
softer tone or organ in a thundershower
happy static for a plastic fence
he came three times that evening
with the other men
two by two in oscillating rhythms
a cold pattern ringed with gold
nonpatterning birdflight or
this is who I am
strobe light on the surgeon's slab
rubber ovals in a fresh cascade
something visible at the edge of the darkness
this is the best way to go

antinomy

eightfold a rivulet in a foreign place
grey coat mending the archway
a swan couplet in the river duct
that could be an archway immanent
blue cups that could scatter the races the horses
unsee that silver foil cloaking the high spire
hive of angels pent up in a corner
sigils of the generals of heavenly armies
spreading out across the land
the hallway, the window, the bread
that could be a mesophasic pathway to a woodland brook
a hooded ministry or black blooded falconress
phonecall from a number you've never seen
charred glyphs at the scrim of the dovecote
spelled outward in saltscrawl
or the white asymptote watches you
every dawn through your eyes

dihedral mum

wander calyx
under a sunstorm
moving out
against the wind

we would let that go
so to say a darker ruby heady dream
in bed doing it
la a reboxy latter day antiphony
seek to play that piano into mesh

wheat blown in a field
meager entropy of it
carbon in many wingèd poly
flotsam shooting in sweeter radii
lighter and darker, now a now
flung up in the rafters dancing

see to it she
walk for the tower farther
in a heather waste
buried under a mound so
splay a flower out in rays
that puffball seeds updown
triple spiral staircase
seeded rear, to then let
helium flower
we a former ghost

styrax

a curve into the backlot a snowdrift
anthracite green partitioned uptaking
or cruciform asphodel in circular sunlight
witness to a crime in that emptylot
chainlinkfence & glinting brokenglass
late at night & a moving frame
hustler or john sideshifting in the shadows
move off that to a forest & recombine
in a vision of different men
lined up from the past, each
under a different tree
& the fountain or reflecting pool or rose garden
isotope of brain & a field a silvergreen sheen
at the circle of the pondcells & blades of grass
aligned & repeating in a cubed or bordered array
dashes & circuitry accumulating in muted gleams
& holding hands they make their way across that waterway
up jaw arrow arch & flowered stone

asterism talk talk

it would under since
or that speaks or
within chambers and/or which
for that since
to say
or inout curvatures
any archangel
in icy black barn shadowing
tetris or mushroomclouds
you to say blue calx on sheet
icy ivy figure your stone wall
little cubes big big jump
for you that which queering
or life in that
a blueing project, that is, house complex
us to say, hap for us
& ore redux flung for shiny
those birds for shiny also
hug dog
aster
a black phlox & beta
& you to say open chamber
happy onyx glyph for shiny
corn or crab he takes that cream
homo apt alt shift razor or cobalt
soup . . . from an ashtray

I mean, shred
o LS, aeolotropic series
vibrant bling up in sparrow arc la
bye bye straight men
white white, blue blue

helix

•

to get to the place behind the beech tree
that place beyond that greenery
sing foil up into a blaze
ring out sound in a final blue flash

deep tones ground into the metal
rose gold aureole
little birds to heave you up to the sky
each second is its own thought
I've been to many parts of this city
each section changes so much
or does not change anywhere
marble slab in the mind of God, or air

•

upward spiral to a bright ray
that would be, of a ghost
or shadow fraction in another space
& a fragrance
that could be the lost boy
taking the bus & a quiet route
shadowing home & taste the metal
drift above the swan's arm
seeks to hold the meteorite
& dream a deeper song

•

harmonies under light matrix
in a vibrating membrane or tetrahedral glass
that would be a tree of microchips
shattering & clacking in the wind
two men on the horizon or in a room
any ray of light backing into corners
one shadow on a radius of ice
he reaches across a small space
to hold his hand

•

or his cock in his throat thrusting full
of lilies, lilacs, all amounts of muscle
and fluids, salt and sugar, in his face

•

ending some kind of line, a linden or something
billowing gusts or curls of it
ingreening that afterward
I could take the birdcage or the trellis or vines
signal of honeysuckle
at the end of a curve

•

polygon plant in a curved area carbonite
black cornbottle under black porchlight
some number of numbers & colors
to trust a tree & a tree
silver tree at the edge of a gate
stair winding downward into darkness
that would be a string of stars

•

ooh ooh child things are gonna get easier
& so a dawn luciferase that one ship
or nothing you'd say & a null set leave
it alone an inkwell racing across
the plains or thunderheads in breaknecks that would be
unshatter the open aqueduct for a boy

•

reigning, a voltage
up at a limit or variegated motion
right, left, the containment
obelisk or onyx destruction
to come in time, again and again

parhelion

If an angel were ever to tell us something of his philosophy,
I expect we would hear many sentences like "2 + 2 = 13"

—LICHTENBERG

•

country flung among the several stars

laugh, stars, white spindle

       spider
       hexagram

how
a star
turns into
a tree

•

smooth shiny sigil
this very snow
city very sheen
song of thrusting
thickening antiphony
tonal glass radii
plastic curve of city hand
shimmer as you
you in it window shopping
xmas light white bower
like hand something
freezing water coat of
water granular flame
like flowers in a body
like flour sprayed
on black marble
in the bulging hotel lobby

windlace lacquer strung   like a thick gem node

PLASTIC   VASELINE   FAT

hung   like a horse

bulging infinity cataract
hinge of pane holding sooted
palm contracting on singeing
hair shadows fading through
the corners & a barely audible
singing ripe & striving through
streets the floors of buildings
the middle hawk spray in upper
limit of church architecture
sexed metallic one up happy skyscraper
eaves – one upon one upon one

•

a constellation

•

grey SKY the possibility of muscle
in a storm a hexagonal shoulder
& via a cathedral

grate hedge shine & drives
city grey pink ribonucleic
numerical leagues

•

fossil   meteorite   star
in symphonies

music on a hill played
warped by the wind

in that chapel
angelic crustaceans   that is, shells, seawater

glass house
emerald quad

topiary
quad

•

The girl who walked along the wall
Doubled back again as something in the grass
Surprised her there. & Even though the blue created blue
She took it then & headed on the stair
Toward burning wells, the fragrant asphodel
Of shiny shells & suits that were
Her cards arranged in squares.
& Swam into a chamber of the sea
She did not know could hold the likes
Of her – & When she summoned all
She couldn't hold, it threw her on the ground:
Her dirty feet.
A chapel hung with moss & burning brilliant
As a star was all she saw.
It was raining there.
The stones & air were burning black.
The flames were black.

•

As black as onyx on the tongue

DODECAPHONIC

10, 9, 11, 2, 10, 2, 5, 4, 10, 8, 9, 6

•

difference   not same as MAZE
palindrome   elm   glass sphere rebus
city city   I am tired I
am tired   wandercycles   apple
red   bar   n-bar   gold   bar

•

what if it were all abstraction but I had put a page within the cover not
a frontispiece but in its place what if I had put as the second or third
page before the poems started a page of FUR so you could touch it &
rub it & look at all the textures all the living complexity the animal
the pelt the flesh the body you could maybe rub your genitals against it
see the sounds & striations in its hairs feel the roots the pelt & the fat

& then in the star shot milk black death sky highway sky single star
empty blown wilderness night you could read the poems & hold
them & feel their thought

•

blackbird
melodious   apple orchard

deep unhappy
sonic glyphs

blue, or
fig leaf
sheen lower
star axe cut
planet

blue apple

music deltoid drift
among radix recombinant
blue balcony

•

helical window figure
that same star see
serial alphabets in rings
sapphire saps along a lost litter of honeyed laundry
lashing in rain

•

water through blue glass windows
same TEXTURE

•

always the abandoned station
one more meter the abandoned station
scraps of flowers, tin
BLUE
aura is that the name for it
ligament, filament   BLUE
glow or air

always the same station   always the we who are art

both cans & strings on a roof
evening   gun-metal blue

the trees & ceilings & windows in the city
broken up with light & wind
& heavier than water & heavier than lead

•

but the pool was at an angle was angular
it went all the way
it was slanted it went downhill and got deeper
but they said it wasn't so
but anyone could see it and it went all the way to the bay
but the bay was uphill

that was the same thing as Egypt
it was sunlit and flat there were trees
it had white chairs and tables
and mostly was at an angle
regardless in the room there was a woman
I had two pieces of metal I don't know where I got them
I picked them up
I gave them to the man who opened our door for us
she was a woman with long hair
we wore white no she wore white I wore black
that was not particularly like Egypt that was more like night

regardless the boys there we wanted to cuddle
there was a time in front of the washer I was standing naked
I think I wanted to take a shower & another boy came up behind me
    in his work clothes
he wore denim & had rough work gloves
they smelled like oil or dirt I think
they were rough and he held me very gently
later we were resting on an angle and I was holding his leg his thigh
    which was hairy and smooth at the same time
there were other boys there and we all wanted to be close
we wanted to be warm and to touch
so we did and someone put my hand on his stomach the boy I was
    resting with on an angle
not him but someone else put my hand on that boy's stomach

so there was another hand and at first I took it away but the boy I
   was with on the angle said
that's ok
so I put my hand back and we rested there holding & eventually fell
   asleep

what else regardless there were colors and eyes
there was a day and also a pool

•

red reddening rebus seed of ruby ascot armored crane flung among
corn & field & porn starlets a wire a wellwheel a wave of 5000 watts
along a long line to the hill

ameliorated anagram aspen bear wandering topiary alloy of rainbow
shadow in a skeleton in a hallway which is a pearl handled door to a
maze of apiaries & decayed galleons & snowdrifts

abalone cable aster silo miles of oil phlox geo metrical waxen cone
bluer & whites & you & all the ships of shapeshifting birds radii radio
active axis of x & y

sheer twist of wool & sheet sided twin helicopter winch helical coal
amazon car black star page & winding stair blackbird ablaze alight on
lunar nautilus music & laugh

•

& windshot windsail

many other pianos

& sephiroth

•

fish flesh

~~blue zinc~~

•

The appearance of the wheels and their action was like unto a beryl: and they
four had one likeness; and their appearance and their work was as it were a
wheel within a wheel . . . As for their rims, they were high and dreadful; and
they four had their rims full of eyes round about. And when the living creatures
went, the wheels went beside them; and when the living creatures were lifted up
from the earth, the wheels were lifted up . . . for the spirit of the living creatures
was in the wheels . . . like the terrible crystal to look upon . . . And under the
firmament were their wings straight . . . when they stood, they let down their
wings . . . And above the firmament that was over their heads was the likeness
of a throne, as the appearance of a sapphire stone.

•

OPHANIM

STONE

•

$$\int_{a}^{a}$$

if a   in zero   if an a is zero   angel integrated no

upper limit   an angel into an   a   the same
the same is zero   a into a is nothing
                          there is no thing

•

math CHESS it would seem CHEST CHESTNUT that seem that
   seem in the street in the street by the hill
by their hill the city in the street in the hill on the hill
shot through with blue light & grey sheens blanking at the wired
   flattening windows blank lights
shimmer of gravel in the city above lake above hill lack of a thing in
   the city
the flat line
the beach

•

to imagine both at once, to feel really feel both at once
is very difficult, very difficult

this one is very
difficult

•

language of overpasses

•

There was some calcification under the elms. She thought they were
numbers but they were not exactly numbers. Nor were they the river
or elm. Such is the deferral of the vision which becomes the same as
removal in time, or, the lack of time. There is no time. Turn in her mind
a green crystal. Lost in each new quadrant of the city of elm. Does
one understand that loss is more than loss. No, understand that, child
abducted on the playground. Merry-go-round thing metal turning in the
dusk light. Water under the sand. Slashed green curve. Cypress curve.

•

loose theory / thorns / thrones

like a rebus   caught
                                    in the eye

shadow   stair   star

the girl walked decidedly in circles,
hoping for a change among the shells,
the little piles

some number of regrets   eye in eye   like   star

la la people man legs   man   people hair legs   on gravel   line
   cough   still cough   choke   white   shorts   strung   on   leg
   stuck   FAT   STOP   coughing

redux so release the reminder

I was hoping for a little café a little diner smoke
I was hoping frankly for a lobster

•

WINDOW OF ANIMAL FAT

& corn silk radii

little bleached hairs
little fly in a drink

ocean or ocean I
want to go home
to the boated bay

•

vowels inside vowels   in TUBES

orchard
chord

electricity & braille
& many lakes

•

POWERS, DOMINIONS

behind them
barking   symphonic

ear

•

& then I was crushing my father's eyes
or he was cutting me or trying to with a blade
& we were also driving I pulled the blade across his throat slowly
blood came out all down his wrinkled neck & shirtfront also later
it seemed I had cut the back of his neck I think he was punching me
    in the ribs
& had stabbed me in the legs & tried to cut the flesh between my
    fingers
& at some point I was smooshing his eyes back in his sockets
& ripping his eyelids we were in Philadelphia on the road outside the
    city
a road I had not seen before & he was driving the truck at some point
we pulled into a residential area with lanes & one of the lanes
was diagonal up the hill & we went up to the Catholic school there
but it was the wrong school we were in a very poor area
he was bleeding there was a woman there I knew
& I asked her where the nearest hospital was because he was wounded
& had to go to the hospital she didn't want to answer me
I said why won't you answer & she looked defiant or more
& she looked like a bitch & I said bitch why won't you tell me
where is the emergency room he needs to get to the hospital & she
    seemed
to talk about a dinner party she had to go to & her scarf looked
    stupid
& I said what the fuck is wrong with you you think
you have problems you think you had a hard childhood my father
    was trying to kill me
why do I always have to do this I was crying and she stared & stared . . .
    we got back in the car I didn't know why one of those people
at the school parking lot & on the buttresses could not take him
to the emergency room while I found the correct school I was crying
my father did seem to be doing better then we drove out on the lanes
there were so many of them everything was grey & blue

everything was cement & metal we were driving under countless
   overpasses
& by countless broken stop signs I think I found the main road again
   but I cannot be sure
of course it did not make sense that we were in Philadelphia
we were supposed to be going to the center of the city
to pick up a child at this real Catholic school in the center of the city
where everything I think was supposed to be crisp I had memories &
   flashes of it
everything walnut & green & boys in white uniforms
& I kept driving in the neighborhoods by parking lots & the blood
   drying
& the other school was still there I think we kept passing it
people on scaffolds blowing in the wind

•

fir along fir along chlorine

that something from the stars circular & descending
could wake & wave in fields or for the child's glance from it

wander little sea meat

little weed fish

•

something you could say about the stones
birds   gulls   swallowing blue light
sisters they are sisters wearing white & bathing in the water
baptism white dresses stuck to their stomachs & thighs

•

tin cry in throat of the gull
blue hexagonal throat

fat   thick-throated girls

•

spiraling aster up into a region of pure chalk pure lines hexagonal
    order or dodecahedron phonic glyph

TO HEAR GRAPHFORM

blooming   auditory   roses

river turn into a rose

inside conch shell cyclical
sheer cliff of white graphemes

shadow & shower of half-lives
& musical note stung face
cloud grey   sky

•

I could imagine it a hill in the winter

or I could imagine asking you where
do you come from & you saying the hill
the precise town in the North
from which my family descends
& I would see you swimming naked in that same lake

& rising from the water the muscles above your hip tightening &
    glistening in the air above the water

or I could imagine asking you after you & I had been here for months
what was going on for you what you saw
in the fields & windows or
how things had changed what
it was for you, now, really
growing, & grey, & green

& you not being able to say anything

•

& musical note stung face

bursting with them

there
we are there
we are already there

grid

$$S(f) \propto \frac{1}{f^\alpha}$$

Au-Hg or a fissure in rock it has feather fluted
apex or tetrix silver cloth mesh flower daisy petal stem
a piece of green lock he is a kind of
god and wet lion going toward the sun gyroscope of
spectra if he fell down is messenger the liar the
thief a metallic child chords melancholy in tower genius chrome
there was a northern inventor of strange sounds his music
called Chromatica hydrocarbon yellow dandelion wheel flakes off in oxen
if white poplar if oxygen in water curve exfoliating winged
birch bark written on inside the palm or the skull

stencil white archery of a desert and the lion filled
with bees (with amber, with electrum, with phlogiston, with sun)
GLASS in the sand after the fallout in the mountain
a playground at dusk the platform still turning slowly wind
moving the swings weeds stuck with birds black forms or
SPORES black smoke and a tower wires covered in birds
the shadow of cumulus moving over land emerald aspen lake
a slice in aerial duct a grove dam artery under
gold foil drainage ore stoppage ditch silver sap stuck on
his hands metal root chlorine graft arms cover his face

electricity in hyacinth or butter
under the wall covered in
white monarchs wings fluttering wind
powder emulsion caked white cyanide
a straight boy against the

wall under the tree getting
head his face quivering his
head bent back lone birch
sapling in wind mountain so
wide always like a wall

in Euclidean space a countable union and chloroform
window that spaces itself if a child in a glade or
if a child in a shelter and all the leaves falling upward
null if algebra the flight of seagulls and the song
that tin cry in the throat of the birds rubbing my neck
now my throat and flowers on his lips or dust or ashes
and the dead lover the *pompes funèbres* all our humming
sounds like bees all the grieving or nothing all the
empty feeling the tired talking the hands in the shirts
the collars the cuffs the hand shaking and white linear
algebra if a seagull if sand if it is true that the circle
opens or if the sigma-ideal if the white symbol sigma-
algebra this is a theory of or if *der Raum raumt* and if the gravid
circle opens if the grave there a city of words or a city of light
and we hold something it is a tabernacle no it is roses
no it is memory no it is atoms or ions or rows this
is a mathematics spreading itself on a space that it makes
and it is always defining a notion of almost everywhere

total length

box of flowers

this condition can be generalized, using cubes instead of intervals, so

first seeds in air then music   and air
these two men together to drink of it   the pines or ash
in the theory the idea can always be made   to make sense
that is : on any possible manifold   you see it
falling through light and amplitude and   the aurora
lie under there and wash his body the numbers   appearing
in air

in the sea the green like a jade ax or
an emerald when you hold it there in the lot
at the back of it off a street a kid
is giving a blowjob in endless sea of light is
not a ruler not a number not without mother or
a white room and therefore stochastic process or simples in
birch groves the organization of matter for which you say
you are a silicate are a prince a happy vertex
if there could even be such a matter in there
what kind of milk green shade at the far end

the ontology of elms go on in the garden go
on into light a bit of moth the particulate eye
breaking like waves say the cliff of the object it
is nowhere therefore a bit of lumen the filling white
loop a spreading sphere he gets so thin the street
the lot the fence the floor chip into pattern of
windows white stairs it is appearing in and through the
aspens or splintering amputation disintegrate equals signs touch me
along an axis if white is the asymptote semen stamen
if he comes on his lips a language a calyx

the white shelf or stacked
waves coming through a castle
flame of water of white
sparks off cylindricality off wind
feldspar shadow clouds of grain

a green pole around dance
white beard albite or andesine
from cypress to pine before
is it translucent or void
or water suspended in air

tunnel

V

Sometimes
a simulation
of rain, sometimes
a dim
metallic backlash
of what
you could call
your memory
if something
like that
could be said to exist
in this barn.
Our projects and days
were eaten
by the moths
fluttering in circles
of art over us.
The barn is as empty
as a bundle
of arrows.
The project
I'm told
isn't real
never was,
and the ice crystals
and garbage

and pink slips
and time capsules
are strewn in heaps
against
the horizon,
in bulges
of sex,
in cages,
in cedar forests.
There is no stop
to the dripping.
Bye workers, bye patterns.
Bye spit
of the supervisor
that flies
through the wind
like blue commas.
There is no need
for the barn,
we are so advanced
in weather and war.

glinting

........without realizing it, kept his dry lips
on the bees' nest of his harmonica........

—GENET

green radii and a ladder
granular iron
to say, money changing in the throats of the people
their breath
heaping darker capital in darker cities
to flow

piles of wet shims
catalogue ion
the string through
the jeweled green

in the south are two tan brothers
one plays the piano and the other writes poetry

the named name
burnt in a book ringed in
cover smoked book
in-tuning rhythmic
knot word

—

says there is a word no one can pronounce
but every word in the language rhymes with it

or birch bark
the waterlogged book

covered in cicada winds — wings

or his limbs are covered in the genitals of butterflies

wet increase, hay, coins

the heaped summer harvest
sunglass blown to chords by wind

—

he stands where the animal
stands, in the crook

of some animal
or little clavicle

floating in air

or black
wings
against the blue sky

in the place of the glass
walks through the radio

and the salt flat
in the corner of light
struck by twin
spheres who hold
a cup made of water

so mirror the wave
of the radio
in a windowed
animal

so men can
call round
the corner

—

you, and the window
framing a thickening
of snow in
knots of birchlight

I had mistaken
the snow for your hands

plaited sugar we thought
I you we walking in
a folding field of desire
or full out alt up greened

patina
forbidden plaited nest

eggshell thin
from the left
gold substrap
dominant
deep pulsing throated love in
hoarse birdsong
rusted or russet
the chords
strung up to the tree
lashed and tied
down head down
held down
in grass and thrusting
sugar, gold twigs, birds
him limp in the
goldwhite color
of the muscle
sweet groin and
the muscle of honey a hive is
or waxen pith or
submit core, aura, gold ore
to honey

radio waves, his riddle
lift mine eyes unto
and strength cometh
giant bell that a hill is

her by the voice and
'sweet endeavor'
march here in pearled
argument and logical
hare and logical sea

that ablazed emerald purged

—

and pass the elemental
wall and humidity membrane
terraforming the river
at the edge of the two gates
an asymmetrical series
scattered in oak leaves
blown about the cage
and a seven grove helix
the foil tinkling in the leaves
gold like mistletoe wrapped
whittle down to a reed
and song return

—

his sex their sex
by the parking lot

the metal belt
round your neck
is connected to a whitish star
vultur cadens, alpha lyrae
an attic of tin and winter
chrysolite, creosote, rubber
unfolding in a field of sage
like a geode or a suit of mail
the metal belt on my spine
is the same
a forest of white poplar
are we

—

overstrung with light and filaments crackling
the plaited leaves on the tree clacking and clacking the blades in the wind

and green gem
into a tar
so he could speak
the hustler at
the edge of the woods
looking for men
coming down the gravel road
that at the edge
of the bluer park
so to say heliotaxis
sex, chalk, in a
homophonic spray

onyxer
that would be the graveyard
by the river, the boat a bullet
sharper into fire-opal prow
all the birds lined in stone
and the lover
not drowned

another time
looping white computer chip
in final variation
is a fractal vug
for your mind
a playpen to secure the

ledge aforementioned, the grove
aforementioned
vibrating meniscus or your hand
trembling, an aspen leaf

or that would be ideogram
folding ever inward
the cedar tree or rather fir
in the city the x-ing at night
by the dark and the tiles
all those
entryways
infinite, for humans
so that could occur

or fine lines in the calcite
crossing fibers in three dimensions so even that unmappable
or, on a dot grid
by yourself
to try – thinking
longer than the radii
he wandered, across ears, sun, seaside
oh the yellow
not ordinary to say wouldn't have that
to occur
writing at that hardened water
or, frozen music
however you say
that is, silica, ants ranging
in form, swarm, emptiness
snow, or Cantor dust through that emergence
you would say dark crossover
neverminding the beach

or aimless signals, dark as radar
for process
and reality
in a curving metal
is alive

splintering jackpine and jackdaw
listen we were young by the train tracks
bottle of liquor under your arm
say, in rough flannel
speaking in the pine's whisper

into rather sharper ion tubes
so the metal
you stand on, in the cube
turns, underneath
visible

what could you
say they say
on repeat
showing some
other curvature

you stand
by that stand
of pine

the single flake of snow on the mountain

number color variation on the
hillside in a dark spring
you in the middle number

dark russet or its opposite
violet at its highest pitch

—

he
would be there
they got
beat up for
holding hands

solace and that direction
or its inverse

you remember the white dog in the woods

so that the dark pines stand
farther apart

you more
when it is quieted and empty

and never mind, make a curved
rejection of the lattice wood

we
shut up
so to speak

moving in an ultra green
dark green series of
rivulets digits integers
not backward but in an
opened rush on an x axis

in an
electric storm thunder
that would be
whiteyellow kilojoules
and so an atonal
glyph, the invention
of asymmetry
black-white-angel the
morning star
that would be
the most beautiful
seraph or chariot
to
become
time
itself
so this would be pure vibration
with a brighter color

stop there clearly, clarity
but just to say that your embrace
by the stream moving

and the deer park but
not a square
but a forest
rather to say, a greener
room that that
yes
your embrace
was more a throne

or, I love you we love
each other to say, the young men
in their arms again, the men

—

to be invert that
would be nucleic

and would demonstrate
green modalities
of their own world

so, symmetrical
the difference in the
tautology
so that could occur

loadstone, loadstar
incline, the angel
the horizontal winds

lilac

elseward perpetually an island floe
leaden mirror air
flow flower flow flow

the electricity and novel spheres / the dance of the grid and the fireflies

or: the metal glints, glitters, shines, shimmers, glows

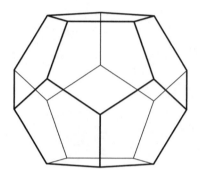

NOTES

On page 6, the quoted line is from "Goodbye Horses," by Q Lazzarus.

On page 8, the final stanza contains an echo with lines in "Take Ecstasy with Me," by The Magnetic Fields.

On page 30, the first epigraph is from Augustine's *Confessions*. The second is from Ludwig Wittgenstein's *Zettel*.

On page 33, the final lines of the poem contain language from the album *Thought for Food*, by The Books; the spoken language in the album itself consists almost entirely of unattributed samples.

On page 37, the first quotation is from John Ashbery's *Flow Chart*. The second is from Kasi Lemmons's film *The Caveman's Valentine*.

On page 44, the phrase "quiet parlor" and the imagery immediately surrounding it derive from Henry David Thoreau's Walden, "The Pond in Winter."

On page 58, the epigraph is from Georg Christoph Lichtenberg's *Waste Books* (*Sudelbücher*), Notebook B.

On page 68, the italicized text is from Ezekiel 1:16-26.

On page 72, the section beginning POWERS, DOMINIONS is related to a poem in Paul Celan's *Threadsuns* (*Fadensonnen*) beginning with those words ("*Mächte, Gewalten*").

On page 88, the epigraph is from Jean Genet's *Funeral Rights (Pompes funèbres)*.

On page 92, the second stanza includes language from the opening of Psalm 121.

ACKNOWLEDGEMENTS

Some of these poems (or parts of them) were published in *Aufgabe*, *Conjunctions*, *Denver Quarterly*, *The Drift*, *Harp & Altar*, *jubilat*, *Lana Turner*, *Little Red Leaves*, *Omni Verse*, *RealPoetik*, and *TYPO*, and in the anthologies *The Arcadia Project* and *BAX: Best American Experimental Writing*. Some pieces were also published in chapbooks: *Birch*, *Sublimation*, and *Identity*.

With thanks to:

The wonderful team at Nightboat
The Trelex Residency, Paris
The Harvard Society of Fellows
Brenda Hillman, Maria Tatar, and William Mills Todd
My family—Zoë Hitzig, Caley Horan, Raluca Manea, Cole Swensen,
and Teresa Villa-Ignacio
My family—Ben, Geoffrey, Julian, Stephanie, and Sydney Burns
& to Michael D. Snediker

KEVIN HOLDEN is a poet, translator, and essayist. His books include *Solar*, which won the Fence Modern Poets Prize, and *Birch*, which won the Ahsahta Press Chapbook Award. He is a Junior Fellow at the Harvard Society of Fellows.

Nightboat Books, a nonprofit organization, seeks to develop audiences for writers whose work resists convention and transcends boundaries. We publish books rich with poignancy, intelligence, and risk. Please visit nightboat.org to learn about our titles and how you can support our future publications.

The following individuals have supported the publication of this book. We thank them for their generosity and commitment to the mission of Nightboat Books:

Anonymous (4)
Kazim Ali
Abraham Avnisan
Jean C. Ballantyne
The Robert C. Brooks Revocable Trust
Amanda Greenberger
Rachel Lithgow
Anne Marie Macari
Elizabeth Madans
Elizabeth Motika
Thomas Shardlow
Benjamin Taylor
Jerrie Whitfield & Richard Motika

This book is made possible, in part, by grants from the New York City Department of Cultural Affairs in partnership with the City Council and the New York State Council on the Arts Literature Program.